Pearls of Peace
A Rosary Journey through the Holy Land

by Christine Haapala
Holy Land Photography by Rev. Gary Coulter

Suffering Servant Scriptorium
Fairfax, VA
www.sufferingservant.com

Nihil Obstat: Rev. Thomas J. Lehning, STL, PhD
             Censor Librorum

Imprimatur: + Paul S. Loverde
               Bishop of Arlington
               January 25, 2012
               Feast of the Conversion of St. Paul, Apostle

Scripture excerpts from the New American Bible with Revised New Testament and Psalms Copyright © 1991, 1986, 1970 by the Confraternity of Christian Doctrine, Washington, D.C. Used with permission. All Rights Reserved. No part of the New American Bible may be reproduced in any form without permission in writing from the copyright owner.

Holy Land Photography, Rev. Gary Coulter, Diocese of Lincoln. Holy Land pilgrimages in 2007 and 2010. © 2007, 2010 G. Coulter. All rights reserved. Used with permission. www.frcoulter.com

The St. Paul Scripture selections in the Joyful, Sorrowful, and Glorious mysteries were originally published as the Sixth Scriptural Rosary in From Genesis to Revelation: Seven Scriptural Rosaries. (ISBN: 0-931886-64-6, 1996; Revised Edition: ISBN: 0-9703996-4-2, 2002)

Cover design, book layout, and map design by Alison Ujueta.

Copyright © 1996, 2002, 2012. Christine Haapala. All Rights Reserved.

ISBN: 978-0-9840394-1-8

Manufactured in United States of America.

Dedicated to
Our Lady of Mount Carmel

Main Altar, Our Lady of Mount Carmel Monastery Haifa

Index of Photography by Location

- **Abu Gosh (Emmaus)**
  - Church of Our Lady of the Ark of the Covenant ... 82
- **Bethany**
  - Church of Lazarus ... 66
- **Bethlehem**
  - Church of the Nativity ... 12, 13, 16
  - Milk Grotto ... 3
  - Shepherds' Field Church ... 14, 15
- **Cana** ... 29
  - Shrine of the First Miracle ... 30
- **Ein Karem** ... 8
  - Church of St. John the Baptist ... 24
  - Church of the Visitation ... 9, 10, 11, 79
- **Haifa**
  - Our Lady of Mount Carmel Monastery ... iii
- **Jerusalem**
  - Basilica of the Agony ... 47
  - Basilica of the Dormition ... 22, 72, 76, 77, 78, 81
  - Cenacle (Upper Room) ... 38, 39, 40, 74
  - Chapel of the Ascension ... 69, 71
  - Church of the Condemnation and Imposition of the Cross ... 56, 59
  - Church of the Flagellation ... 50
  - Church of the Holy Sepulchre ... 60 61, 62, 64, 65
  - Church of the Pater Noster ... 53, 84
  - Church of St. Peter in Gallicantu ... 44, 49, 52
  - Dominus Flevit Church ... 41
  - Garden of Gethsemane ... 46
  - Hillside to Jericho ... 18
  - Notre Dame Center ... vii
  - Outside Jerusalem (Dromedary) ... 20
  - Panorama of Jerusalem ... 42, 43
  - Via Dolorosa ... 45, 55, 57, 58
  - Western Wall of the Ancient Jewish Temple ... 19
- **Jordan River** ... 23, 25
- **Kursi** ... 33
- **Mount of Temptation**
  - Monastery of the Temptation ... 27
- **Mount Tabor**
  - Church of the Transfiguration ... 37
  - Site of the Transfiguration ... 35
- **Nazareth**
  - Basilica of the Annunciation ... 4, 6, 7, 28, 63
  - St. Joseph Church ... 2
- **Tiberias**
  - Church of St. Peter ... 21, 75
- **Sea of Galilee** ... vi
  - Church of the Beatitudes ... 34
  - Mount of the Beatitudes ... 31
  - Tabgha ... 32
    - Church of the Primacy of Peter ... 68

Sea of Galilee
The Source of the Jordan River

Journey of a Lifetime

Going on a pilgrimage can at first seem to have some similarities to a vacation. It means departing from the normal routine of our everyday lives. It involves traveling to some destination. But what makes a pilgrimage isn't just the travel, or even the destination. What is important is that it is also a spiritual journey. On a pilgrimage, we might visit a holy place or a Church, we might visit the relics of a saint or a famous shrine. But ultimately, all such places and people remind us that the destination of our pilgrimage, the pilgrimage of our lives, is Jesus Christ!

Pilgrimages are a long tradition in the Church, in many ways following the example of the Magi, the wise men in the 2nd chapter of the Gospel of Matthew who traveled, searching for the newborn king, and when they arrived in Jerusalem they proclaimed: "We have come to adore him." We too search for Jesus Christ, we seek to do him homage. Thus the Mass is a special part of that journey of our lives, for we do not have to travel great distances to encounter Jesus Christ, to worship Him in the Eucharist, to acknowledge Him as our Creator, our only Lord and Savior, to give Him pride of place in our lives.

Every pilgrim learns that the journey is not always easy, pilgrimage always involves some difficulties and inconvenience. Yet even more we learn that following after Christ is not easy either. On the path of conversion and repentance, the journey we take always leads us to the cross. "If anyone wishes to come after me, he must deny himself and take up his cross daily and follow me." *Lk 9:23*

Notre Dame Center Jerusalem

Thus every pilgrimage ultimately is to be a reminder that we are pilgrims here on earth, this world is not our final home. No, we are journeying towards our home of heaven, our final goal is Jesus Christ. To him be honor and glory forever. Amen.

Rev. Gary Coulter
Diocese of Lincoln

www.frcoulter.com

Table of Contents

Dedication Page iii
Holy Land and Surrounding Regions iv
Index of Photography by Location v
"Journey of a Lifetime" by Rev. Gary Coulter vii

Pearls of Peace 1

The Joyful Mysteries 3
    The Annunciation 4
    The Visitation 8
    The Nativity 12
    The Presentation of Jesus in the Temple 16
    The Finding of Jesus in the Temple 19

The Luminous Mysteries 23
    The Baptism of Jesus 24
    The Wedding at Cana 28
    The Proclamation of the Kingdom 31
    The Transfiguration 35
    The Institution of the Eucharist 38

Psalm 122 42

The Sorrowful Mysteries 45
    The Agony in the Garden 46
    The Scourging at the Pillar 50
    The Crowning with Thorns 53
    The Carrying of the Cross 56
    The Crucifixion 60

The Glorious Mysteries 65
    The Resurrection 66
    The Ascension 69
    The Descent of the Holy Spirit 72
    The Assumption of the Blessed Virgin Mary into Heaven 76
    The Coronation of Mary, Queen of Heaven and Earth 79

Notes from the Author 83
How to Pray the Most Holy Rosary 85
The Prayers of the Most Holy Rosary 85

Pearls of Peace
A Rosary Journey
through the Holy Land

*Statue of the Holy Family
St. Joseph Church, Nazareth*

The Joyful Mysteries

The Sign of the Cross

The Apostles' Creed

[T]he fruit of the Spirit is love, joy, peace. *Gal 5:22*

Our Father...

Keep the faith [that] you have to yourself in the presence of God. *Rom 14:22*

Hail Mary...

[Abraham] believed, hoping against hope, that he would become "the father of many nations," according to what was said, "Thus shall your descendants be." *Rom 4:18*

Hail Mary...

Let love be sincere; hate what is evil, hold on to what is good; love one another with mutual affection. *Rom 12:9-10*

Hail Mary... Glory Be... O My Jesus...

Altar in the Milk Grotto
Bethlehem

The First Joyful Mystery
The Annunciation

[T]he angel Gabriel was sent from God to a town of Galilee called Nazareth, to a virgin betrothed to a man named Joseph, of the house of David, and the virgin's name was Mary. ... "Glory to God in the highest / and on earth peace to those on whom his favor rests." Lk 1:26-27, Lk 2:14

Our Father...

"Behold, I am the handmaid of the Lord." Lk 1:38
Basilica of the Annunciation, Nazareth

[W]e speak God's wisdom, mysterious, hidden. *1 Cor 2:7*

Hail Mary...

For those he foreknew he also predestined to be conformed to the image of his Son, so that he might be the firstborn among many brothers. *Rom 8:29*

Hail Mary...

In him you also, who have heard the word of truth, the gospel of your salvation, and have believed in him, were sealed with the promised holy Spirit. *Eph 1:13*

Hail Mary...

Now the one who has prepared us for this very thing is God, who has given us the Spirit as a first installment. *2 Cor 5:5*

Hail Mary...

Do you not know that if you present yourselves to someone as obedient slaves, you are slaves of the one you obey, either of sin, which leads to death, or of obedience, which leads to righteousness? *Rom 6:16*

Hail Mary...

For just as through the disobedience of one person the many were made sinners, so through the obedience of one the many will be made righteous. *Rom 5:19*

Hail Mary...

For while your obedience is known to all, so that I rejoice over you, I want you to be wise as to what is good, and simple as to what is evil. *Rom 16:19*

Hail Mary...

In him we were also chosen, destined in accord with the purpose of the One who accomplishes all things according to the intention of his will, so that we might exist for the praise of his glory, we who first hoped in Christ. *Eph 1:11-12*

Hail Mary...

[A] virgin is anxious about the things of the Lord, so that she may be holy in both body and spirit. *1 Cor 7:34*

Hail Mary...

And the Word became flesh... Jn 1:14
Altar at the Grotto of the Annunciation
Basilica of the Annunciation, Nazareth

Do you not know that your body is a temple of the holy Spirit within you, whom you have from God, and that you are not your own?
1 Cor 6:19

Hail Mary... Glory Be... O My Jesus...

Our Lady of Vladimir, Protectress of Russia
Basilica of the Annunciation, Nazareth

The Second Joyful Mystery
The Visitation

During those days Mary set out and traveled to the hill country in haste to a town of Judah, where she entered the house of Zechariah and greeted Elizabeth. … As you enter a house, wish it peace. *Lk 1:39-40, Mt 10:12*

Our Father...

Site of the Visitation
Home of Zechariah and Elizabeth
Ein Karem

[W]e walk by faith, not by sight … "How beautiful are the feet of those who bring [the] good news!" *2 Cor 5:7, Rom 10:15*

Hail Mary...

Franciscan Church of the Visitation
Southern hill above Ein Karem

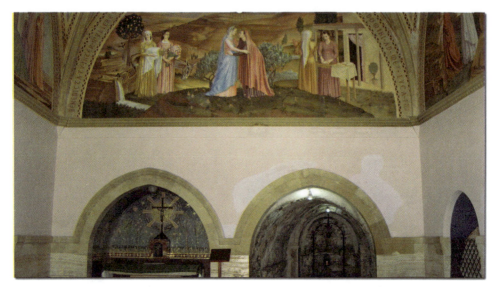

" Most blessed are you among women..." Lk 1:42
Painting of Elizabeth greeting Mary
Church of the Visitation, Ein Karem

Greet one another with a holy kiss. All the holy ones greet you.
2 Cor 13:12

Hail Mary...

Rejoice always. Pray without ceasing. In all circumstances give thanks, for this is the will of God for you in Christ Jesus. *1 Thes 5:16-18*

Hail Mary...

[M]ay the Lord make you increase and abound in love for one another and for all, just as we have for you. *1 Thes 3:12*

Hail Mary...

[E]ncourage one another, agree with one another, live in peace, and the God of love and peace will be with you. 2 Cor 13:11

Hail Mary...

Contribute to the needs of the holy ones, exercise hospitality. Rom 12:13

Hail Mary...

Put on then, as God's chosen ones, holy and beloved, heartfelt compassion, kindness, humility, gentleness, and patience. *Col 3:12*

Hail Mary...

We who are strong ought to put up with the failings of the weak and not to please ourselves; let each of us please our neighbor for the good, for building up. *Rom 15:1-2*

Hail Mary...

[W]hile we have the opportunity, let us do good to all, but especially to those who belong to the family of the faith. *Gal 6:10*

Hail Mary...

[S]erve one another through love. For the whole law is fulfilled in one statement, namely, "You shall love your neighbor as yourself." *Gal 5:13-14*

Hail Mary... Glory Be... O My Jesus...

" My soul proclaims the greatness of the Lord..." Lk 1:46
Church of the Visitation, Ein Karem

The Third Joyful Mystery
The Nativity

For today in the city of David a savior has been born for you who is Messiah and Lord. ... Prince of Peace. His dominion is vast / and forever peaceful. ... When Jesus was born in Bethlehem of Judea, in the days of King Herod, behold, magi from the east arrived in Jerusalem, saying, "Where is the newborn king of the Jews?"
Lk 2:11, Is 9:5-6, Mt 2:1-2

Our Father...

Church of the Nativity
Bethlehem

"A savior has been born..." Lk 2:11
The Grotto
Church of the Nativity, Bethlehem

Pay to all their dues, taxes to whom taxes are due, toll to whom toll is due, respect to whom respect is due, honor to whom honor is due. *Rom 13:7*

Hail Mary...

[S]he will be saved through motherhood, provided women persevere in faith and love and holiness, with self-control. *1 Tm 2:15*

Hail Mary...

As proof that you are children, God sent the spirit of his Son into our hearts, crying out, "Abba, Father!" *Gal 4:6*

Hail Mary...

[W]hen the fullness of time had come, God sent his Son, born of a woman, born under the law, to ransom those under the law, so that we might receive adoption. *Gal 4:4-5*

Hail Mary...

[H]e emptied himself, / taking the form of a slave, / coming in human likeness; / and found human in appearance ... Because of this, God greatly exalted him / and bestowed on him the name / that is above every name. *Phil 2:7,9*

Hail Mary...

"The deliverer will come out of Zion, / he will turn away godlessness from Jacob; / and this is my covenant with them / when I take away their sins." *Rom 11:26-27*

Hail Mary...

[T]here were shepherds ... keeping the night watch over their flock. ... The angel of the Lord appeared to them... Lk 2:8-9
Painting, Shepherds' Field Church, Bethlehem

[H]e will fall down and worship God, declaring, "God is really in your midst." *1 Cor 14:25*

Hail Mary...

[L]ove from a pure heart, a good conscience, and a sincere faith. *1 Tm 1:5*

Hail Mary...

[N]ot because of any righteous deeds we had done / but because of his mercy, / he saved us through the bath of rebirth / and renewal by the holy Spirit. *Ti 3:5*

Hail Mary...

[I]f you belong to Christ, then you are Abraham's descendant, heirs according to the promise. *Gal 3:29*

Hail Mary... Glory Be... O My Jesus...

Shepherds' Field Church, Bethlehem

The Fourth Joyful Mystery
The Presentation of Jesus in the Temple

When the days were completed for their purification according to the law of Moses, they took him up to Jerusalem to present him to the Lord. ... When they had fulfilled all the prescriptions..., they returned to Galilee, to their own town of Nazareth. ... [T]he peace of God that surpasses all understanding will guard your hearts and minds in Christ Jesus. *Lk 2:22,39, Phil 4:7*

Our Father...

Painting of the Holy Family
Church of the Nativity, Bethlehem

Whoever observes the day, observes it for the Lord. *Rom 14:6*

> *Hail Mary...*

Let every person be subordinate to the higher authorities, for there is no authority except from God, and those that exist have been established by God. *Rom 13:1*

> *Hail Mary...*

Does, then, the one who supplies the Spirit to you and works mighty deeds among you do so from works of the law or from faith in what you heard? *Gal 3:5*

> *Hail Mary...*

So then the law is holy, and the commandment is holy and righteous and good. *Rom 7:12*

> *Hail Mary...*

[W]e do not cease praying for you and asking that you may be filled with the knowledge of his will through all spiritual wisdom and understanding. *Col 1:9*

> *Hail Mary...*

I came ... with a demonstration of spirit and power, so that your faith might rest not on human wisdom but on the power of God. *1 Cor 2:3-5*

> *Hail Mary...*

[O]ne who prophesies does speak to human beings, for their building up, encouragement, and solace. *1 Cor 14:3*

> *Hail Mary...*

In all wisdom and insight, he has made known to us the mystery of his will in accord with his favor that he set forth in him as a plan for the fullness of times, to sum up all things in Christ, in heaven and on earth. *Eph 1:8-10*

Hail Mary...

[W]hatever you do, do everything for the glory of God. *1 Cor 10:31*

Hail Mary...

For if we live, we live for the Lord, and if we die, we die for the Lord; so then, whether we live or die, we are the Lord's. *Rom 14:8*

Hail Mary... Glory Be... O My Jesus...

Hillside along the road from Jerusalem to Jericho (Parable of the Good Samaritan), near the Monastery of St. George

The Fifth Joyful Mystery
The Finding of Jesus in the Temple

For the peace of Jerusalem pray: / ... May peace be within your ramparts. ... [T]he boy Jesus remained behind in Jerusalem. ... Thinking that he was in the caravan, [Mary and Joseph] journeyed for a day and looked for him. ... [T]hey returned to Jerusalem ... [and] found him in the temple. *Ps 122:6-7, Lk 2:43-46*

Our Father...

Western Wall of the Ancient Jewish Temple Jerusalem

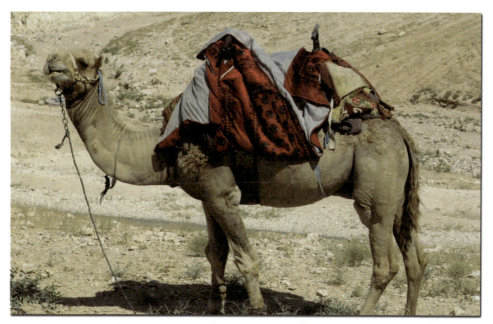
Dromedary outside of Jerusalem

Do you not know that you are the temple of God, and that the Spirit of God dwells in you? *1 Cor 3:16*

Hail Mary...

Let the word of Christ dwell in you richly, as in all wisdom you teach and admonish one another. *Col 3:16*

Hail Mary...

Keep the faith [that] you have to yourself in the presence of God. *Rom 14:22*

Hail Mary...

[Show] yourself as a model of good deeds in every respect, with integrity in your teaching, dignity, and sound speech. *Ti 2:7-8*

Hail Mary...

What thanksgiving, then, can we render to God for you, for all the joy we feel on your account before our God? *1 Thes 3:9*

Hail Mary...

[L]ive in a manner worthy of the Lord, so as to be fully pleasing, in every good work bearing fruit and growing in the knowledge of God.
Col 1:10

Hail Mary...

"Honor your father and mother." This is the first commandment with a promise, "that it may go well with you and that you may have a long life on earth." *Eph 6:2-3*

Hail Mary...

Oh, the depth of the riches and wisdom and knowledge of God! How inscrutable are his judgments and how unsearchable his ways! *Rom 11:33*

Hail Mary...

Children, obey your parents [in the Lord], for this is right. *Eph 6:1*

Hail Mary...

Fathers ... bring them up with the training and instruction of the Lord. *Eph 6:4*

Hail Mary... Glory Be...
O My Jesus...
Hail Holy Queen...

Statue of St. Joseph and the child Jesus Church of St. Peter, Tiberias

"Behold, the Lamb of God." Jn 1:29
St. John the Baptist Chapel, Basilica of the Dormition
Mt Zion, Jerusalem

The Luminous Mysteries

The Sign of the Cross

The Apostles' Creed

The fruit of righteousness is sown in peace for those who cultivate peace. ... For you were once darkness, but now you are light in the Lord. Live as children of light, for light produces every kind of goodness and righteousness and truth. *Jas 3:18, Eph 5:8-9*

Our Father...

I live by faith in the Son of God who has loved me. ... one Lord, one faith, one baptism. ... [S]tand firm in the faith. *Gal 2:20, Eph 4:5, 1 Cor 16:13*

Hail Mary...

[W]e look not for what is seen but to what is unseen ... what is unseen is eternal. ... [I]f we hope for what we do not see, we wait with endurance. *2 Cor 4:18, Rom 8:25*

Hail Mary...

What will separate us from the love of Christ? *Rom 8:35*

Hail Mary... Glory Be... O My Jesus...

Jordan River

The First Luminous Mystery
The Baptism of Jesus

Jesus came from Galilee to John at the Jordan to be baptized by him. … Love and truth will meet; / justice and peace will kiss.
Mt 3:13, Ps 85:11

Our Father...

Painting of the Baptism of Jesus in the Jordan
Church of St. John the Baptist
Ein Karem

[T]he god of this age has blinded the minds of the unbelievers, so that they may not see the light of the gospel of the glory of Christ, who is the image of God. *2 Cor 4:4*

Hail Mary...

Baptisms in the Jordan River

[P]ut on the new self, created in God's way in righteousness and holiness of truth. *Eph 4:24*

Hail Mary...

For all of you were baptized into Christ have clothed yourselves with Christ. ... you are all one in Christ Jesus. *Gal 3:27-28*

Hail Mary...

[Y]ou were also called to the one hope of your call; one Lord, one faith, one baptism; one God and Father of all, who is over all and through all and in all. *Eph 4:4-6*

Hail Mary...

[A]re you unaware that we who were baptized into Christ Jesus were baptized into his death? *Rom 6:3*

Hail Mary...

For in one Spirit we were all baptized into one body ... given to drink of one Spirit. ... [You] have put on the new self, which is being renewed, for knowledge, in the image of its creator. *1 Cor 12:13, Col 3:10*

Hail Mary...

[N]ow you have had yourselves washed, you were sanctified, you were justified in the name of the Lord Jesus Christ and in the Spirit of our God. *1 Cor 6:11*

Hail Mary...

For we do not preach ourselves but Jesus Christ as Lord, and ourselves as your slaves for the sake of Jesus. *2 Cor 4:5*

Hail Mary...

[F]or us there is / one God, the Father, / from whom all things are and for whom we exist, / and one Lord, Jesus Christ, / through whom all things are and through whom we exist. *1 Cor 8:6*

Hail Mary...

Christ loved the church and handed himself over for her to sanctify her, cleansing her by the bath of water with the word, that he might present to himself the church in splendor ... holy and without blemish. *Eph 5:25-27*

Hail Mary... Glory Be... O My Jesus...

*Monastery of the Temptation
Mount of Temptation, near Jericho*

The Second Luminous Mystery
The Wedding At Cana

[T]here was a wedding in Cana in Galilee, and the mother of Jesus was there. ... [T]he wine ran short. ... His mother said to the servers, "Do whatever he tells you." ... Jesus did this as the beginning of his signs in Cana in Galilee. ... There is an appointed time for everything, ... [a] time to love ... and a time of peace. Jn 2:1,3,5,11, Eccl 3:1,8

Our Father...

Painting of the Wedding at Cana
Basilica of the Annunciation, Nazareth

Now there were six stone water jars there for Jewish ceremonial washings, each holding twenty to thirty gallons. Jn 2:6
Cana, Galilee

This is a great mystery … each one of you should love his wife as himself, and the wife should respect her husband. *Eph 5:32-33*

Hail Mary…

[I]f one loves God, one is known by him. *1 Cor 8:3*

Hail Mary…

[T]he fruit of the Spirit is love, joy, peace. *Gal 5:22*

Hail Mary…

[L]ive in a manner worthy of the call you received … bearing with one another through love … *Eph 4:1-2*

Hail Mary…

Love is patient, love is kind. *1 Cor 13:4*

Hail Mary…

[Love] bears all things, believes all things, hopes all things, endures all things. *1 Cor 13:7*

Hail Mary...

Love never fails. *1 Cor 13:8*

Hail Mary...

So faith, hope, love remain, these three; but the greatest of these is love. *1 Cor 13:13*

Hail Mary...

The husband should fulfill his duty toward his wife, and likewise the wife toward her husband. *1 Cor 7:3*

Hail Mary...

And this is my prayer: that your love may increase ever more and more in knowledge ... that you may be pure and blameless for the day of Christ. *Phil 1:9-10*

Hail Mary... Glory Be... O My Jesus...

Jesus and his disciples were also invited to the wedding. Jn 2:2
Shrine of the First Miracle, Cana, Galilee

The Third Luminous Mystery
The Proclamation of the Kingdom

He came and preached peace to you who were far and peace to those who were near. ... Jesus said ... "I have not come to call the righteous to repentance but sinners." ... [H]e went up the mountain. ... [H]e began to teach them, saying: ... "Blessed are the peacemakers, / for they will be called children of God." *Eph 2:17, Lk 5:31-32, Mt 5:1-2, 9*

Our Father...

*Mount of the Beatitudes
Sea of Galilee*

I do not want you to be unaware of this mystery … / "The deliverer will come out of Zion, / he will turn away godlessness from Jacob; / and this is my covenant with them / when I take away their sins." *Rom 11:25-27*

Hail Mary…

[M]y heart's desire and prayer to God on their behalf is for salvation. *Rom 10:1*

Hail Mary…

[N]ow that you have been freed from sin and have become slaves of God, the benefit that you have leads to sanctification, and its end is eternal life. *Rom 6:22*

Hail Mary…

[Y]ou too must think of yourselves as [being] dead to sin and living for God in Christ Jesus. *Rom 6:11*

Hail Mary…

Site of the Multiplication of the Loaves and Fishes at Tabgha

Put on the armor of God so that you may be able to stand firm against the tactics of the devil. *Eph 6:11*

Hail Mary...

In all circumstances, hold faith as a shield, to quench all [the] flaming arrows of the evil one. And take the helmet of salvation and the sword of the Spirit, which is the word of God. *Eph 6:16-17*

Hail Mary...

The demons came out of the man and entered the swine, and the herd rushed down the steep bank into the lake and was drowned. Lk 8:33
Kursi, Territory of the Gerasenes, opposite Galilee

"Blessed are they whose iniquities are forgiven / and whose sins are covered. / Blessed is the man whose sin the Lord does not record." *Rom 4:7-8*

Hail Mary...

For the wages of sin is death, but the gift of God is eternal life in Christ Jesus our Lord. *Rom 6:23*

Hail Mary...

For the law of the spirit of life in Christ Jesus has freed you from the law of sin and death. *Rom 8:2*

Hail Mary...

God will judge people's hidden works through Christ Jesus. *Rom 2:16*

Hail Mary... Glory Be... O My Jesus...

*Franciscan Church of the Beatitudes
Mount of the Beatitudes, Galilee*

The Fourth Luminous Mystery
The Transfiguration

Jesus took Peter, James, and John his brother, and led them up a high mountain by themselves. And he was transfigured before them; his face shone like the sun and his clothes became white as light. ... Grace to you and peace from God our Father and the Lord Jesus Christ. *Mt 17:1-2, 1 Cor 1:3*

Our Father...

*Site of the Transfiguration
Mount Tabor*

Ever since the creation of the world, his invisible attributes of eternal power and divinity have been able to be understood and perceived in what he has made. *Rom 1:20*

> *Hail Mary...*

For God who said, "Let light shine out of darkness," has shone in our hearts to bring to light the knowledge of the glory of God on the face of [Jesus] Christ. *2 Cor 4:6*

> *Hail Mary...*

For you were once darkness, but now you are light in the Lord. Live as children of light, for light produces every kind of goodness and righteousness and truth. *Eph 5:8-9*

> *Hail Mary...*

[A]ll have sinned and are deprived of the glory of God. ... "Awake, O sleeper, / and arise from the dead, / and Christ will give you light." *Rom 3:23, Eph 5:14*

> *Hail Mary...*

He delivered us from the power of darkness and transferred us to the kingdom of his beloved Son, in whom we have redemption, the forgiveness of sins. *Col 1:13-14*

> *Hail Mary...*

[D]o not make any judgment before the appointed time, until the Lord comes, for he will bring to light what is hidden in darkness and will manifest the motives of our hearts.... *1 Cor 4:5*

> *Hail Mary...*

For our salvation is nearer now than when we first believed; the night is advanced, the day is at hand. Let us then throw off the works of darkness [and] put on the armor of light.... *Rom 13:11-12*

> *Hail Mary...*

For in him dwells the whole fullness of the deity bodily, and you share in this fullness in him.... *Col 2:9-10*

Hail Mary...

[O]ur citizenship is in heaven, and from it we also await a savior, the Lord Jesus Christ. He will change our lowly body to conform with his glorified body.... *Phil 3:20-21*

Hail Mary...

For all of you are children of the light and children of the day. ... For from him and through him and for him are all things. To him be glory forever. Amen. *1 Thes 5:5, Rom 11:36*

Hail Mary... Glory Be... O My Jesus...

*Church of the Transfiguration
Mount Tabor*

The Fifth Luminous Mystery
The Institution of the Eucharist

"He will show you a large upper room that is furnished. Make the preparations there." ... Then he took the bread, said the blessing, broke it, and gave it to them, saying, "This is my body, which will be given for you; do this in memory of me." ... Keep on doing what you have learned and received and heard and seen in me. Then the God of peace will be with you. *Lk 22:12,19, Phil 4:9*

Our Father...

Cenacle, the "Last Supper Room" Mount Zion, Jerusalem

Christ loved us and handed himself over for us as a sacrificial offering to God.... *Eph 5:2*

Hail Mary...

For I received from the Lord what I also handed on to you, that the Lord Jesus, on the night he was handed over, took bread, and, after he had given thanks, broke it.... *I Cor 11:23-24*

Hail Mary...

[He] said, "This is my body that is for you. Do this in remembrance of me." *I Cor 11:24*

Hail Mary...

In the same way also the cup, after supper, saying, "This cup is the new covenant in my blood. Do this, as often as you drink it, in remembrance of me." *I Cor 11:25*

Hail Mary...

Franciscan Church of the Cenacle (Upper Room) Jerusalem

*Exterior of the Upper Room
Jerusalem*

For as often as you eat this bread and drink the cup, you proclaim the death of the Lord until he comes. *1 Cor 11:26*

Hail Mary...

[Y]ou are fellow citizens with the holy ones and members of the household of God, built upon the foundation of the apostles and prophets with Christ Jesus himself as the capstone. *Eph 2:19-20*

Hail Mary...

You cannot drink the cup of the Lord and also the cup of demons. You cannot partake of the table of the Lord and of the table of demons. ... Do not grow slack in zeal, be fervent in spirit, serve the Lord. *1 Cor 10:21, Rom 12:11*

Hail Mary...

Through him the whole structure is held together and grows into a temple sacred in the Lord; in him you also are being built together into a dwelling place of God in the Spirit. *Eph 2:21-22*

Hail Mary...

The bread that we break, is it not a participation in the body of Christ? Because the loaf of bread is one, we, though many, are one body, for we all partake of the one loaf. *1 Cor 10:16-17*

Hail Mary...

For our paschal lamb, Christ, has been sacrificed. Therefore, let us celebrate the feast ... with the unleavened bread of sincerity and truth. *1 Cor 5:7-8*

Hail Mary... Glory Be... O My Jesus... Hail Holy Queen...

"I yearned to gather your children together, as a hen gathers her young under her wings, but you were unwilling!" Mt 23:37
Mosaic, Dominus Flevit Church, Jerusalem

I rejoiced when they said to me,
"Let us go to the house of the LORD."
And now our feet are standing
within your gates, Jerusalem.
Jerusalem, built as a city,
walled round about.
Here the tribes have come,
the tribes of the LORD,
As it was decreed for Israel,
to give thanks to the name of the LORD.

Here are the thrones of justice,
the thrones of the house of David.

For the peace of Jerusalem pray:
"May those who love you prosper!
May peace be within your ramparts,
prosperity within your towers."
For family and friends I say,
"May peace be yours."
For the house of the LORD, our God, I pray,
"May blessings be yours." Ps 122:1-9

"Lord, you know everything,
you know that I love you." Jn 21:17
Church of St. Peter in Gallicantu, Jerusalem

The Sorrowful Mysteries

The Sign of the Cross

The Apostles' Creed

For this momentary light affliction is producing for us an eternal weight of glory beyond all comparison. ... Though ... the hills be shaken, / My love shall never leave you / nor my covenant of peace be shaken. *2 Cor 4:17, Is 54:10*

Our Father...

[F]aith comes from what is heard, and what is heard comes through the word of Christ. *Rom 10:17*

Hail Mary...

For this we toil and struggle, because we have set our hope on the living God, who is the savior of all, especially of those who believe. *1 Tm 4:10*

Hail Mary...

Love is patient; love is kind. ... Love never fails. *1 Cor 13:4,8*

Hail Mary... Glory Be... O My Jesus...

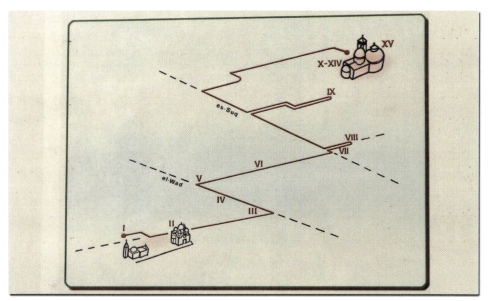

A large crowd of people followed Jesus... Lk 23:27
Beginning of the Via Dolorosa, Jerusalem

The First Sorrowful Mystery
The Agony in the Garden

Jesus went out with his disciples across the Kidron valley to where there was a garden, ... a place named Gethsemane, and he said to his disciples, "Sit here while I pray." ... Do not drag me off with the wicked, / with those who do wrong, / Who speak peace to their neighbors / though evil is in their hearts. *Jn 18:1, Mk 14:32, Ps 28:3*

Our Father...

Garden of Gethsemane
Mount of Olives, Jerusalem

*Rock of the Agony, Basilica of the Agony
(also called Church of All Nations)
At the foot of the Mount of Olives, Jerusalem*

The cup of blessing that we bless, is it not a participation in the blood of Christ? The bread that we break, is it not a participation in the body of Christ? *1 Cor 10:16*

Hail Mary...

Persevere in prayer, being watchful in it with thanksgiving. *Col 4:2*

Hail Mary...

[W]e ourselves, who have the firstfruits of the Spirit, we also groan within ourselves as we wait for adoption, the redemption of our bodies. *Rom 8:23*

Hail Mary...

Blessed be the God and Father of our Lord Jesus Christ, the Father of compassion and God of all encouragement, who encourages us in our every affliction, so that we may be able to encourage those who are in any affliction with the encouragement with which we ourselves are encouraged by God. *2 Cor 1:3-4*

Hail Mary...

[W]e groan, longing to be further clothed with our heavenly habitation. *2 Cor 5:2*

Hail Mary...

In the same way, the Spirit too comes to the aid of our weakness; for we do not know how to pray as we ought, but the Spirit itself intercedes with inexpressible groanings. *Rom 8:26*

Hail Mary...

Have no anxiety at all, but in everything, by prayer and petition, with thanksgiving, make your requests known to God. *Phil 4:6*

Hail Mary...

[P]ray for us, so that the word of the Lord may speed forward and be glorified, as it did among you, and that we may be delivered from perverse and wicked people, for not all have faith. *2 Thes 3:1-2*

Hail Mary...

[T]he night is advanced, the day is at hand. Let us then throw off the works of darkness [and] put on the armor of light. *Rom 13:12*

Hail Mary...

For even when we were among you, we used to warn you in advance that we would undergo affliction. *1 Thes 3:4*

Hail Mary... Glory Be... O My Jesus...

"I do not know him." Lk 22:57
Church of St. Peter in Gallicantu
Mount Zion, Jerusalem

The Second Sorrowful Mystery
The Scourging at the Pillar

[The Jews] brought Jesus from Caiaphas to the praetorium. ... Pilate took Jesus and had him scourged. ... For he is our peace, he ... broke down the dividing wall of enmity, through his flesh. *Jn 18:28, Jn 19:1, Eph 2:14*

Our Father...

*Church of the Flagellation
Old City Jerusalem*

He who did not spare his own Son but handed him over for us all, how will he not also give us everything else along with him? *Rom 8:32*

Hail Mary...

If we are afflicted, it is for your encouragement and salvation; if we are encouraged, it is for your encouragement, which enables you to endure the same sufferings that we suffer. *2 Cor 1:6*

Hail Mary...

But if we hope for what we do not see, we wait with endurance. *Rom 8:25*

Hail Mary...

Five times at the hands of the Jews I received forty lashes minus one. Three times I was beaten with rods. *2 Cor 11:24-25*

Hail Mary...

Miserable one that I am! Who will deliver me from this mortal body? *Rom 7:24*

Hail Mary...

In all circumstances, hold faith as a shield, to quench all [the] flaming arrows of the evil one. *Eph 6:16*

Hail Mary...

[B]e firm, steadfast, always fully devoted to the work of the Lord, knowing that in the Lord your labor is not in vain. *1 Cor 15:58*

Hail Mary...

[A]ffliction produces endurance, and endurance, proven character, and proven character, hope. *Rom 5:3-4*

Hail Mary...

[H]ope does not disappoint, because the love of God has been poured out into our hearts through the holy Spirit that has been given to us.
Rom 5:5

Hail Mary...

The Lord will rescue me from every evil threat and will bring me safe to his heavenly kingdom. To him be glory forever and ever. Amen.
2 Tm 4:18

Hail Mary... Glory Be... O My Jesus...

*Relief of the Arrest of Jesus
Church of St. Peter in Gallicantu
(House of Caiaphas)
Jerusalem*

The Third Sorrowful Mystery
The Crowning with Thorns

[T]he soldiers wove a crown out of thorns and placed it on his head, and ... said "Hail, King of the Jews!" ... Pilate ... brought Jesus out and seated him on the judge's bench in the place called Stone Pavement, in Hebrew, Gabbatha. ... Justice will bring about peace; / right will produce calm and security. *Jn 19:2-3,13, Is 32:17*

Our Father...

And the soldiers wove a crown out of thorns... Jn 19:2
Spina Christi Tree
Church of the Pater Noster, Jerusalem

[W]e groan and are weighed down, because we do not wish to be unclothed but to be further clothed, so that what is mortal may be swallowed up by life. *2 Cor 5:4*

Hail Mary...

Am I now currying favor with human beings or God? Or am I seeking to please people? *Gal 1:10*

Hail Mary...

Who will bring a charge against God's chosen ones? It is God who acquits us. *Rom 8:33*

Hail Mary...

Bless those who persecute [you], bless and do not curse them. Rejoice with those who rejoice, weep with those who weep. *Rom 12:14-15*

Hail Mary...

[W]e were utterly weighed down beyond our strength, so that we despaired even of life. Indeed, we had accepted within ourselves the sentence of death, that we might trust not in ourselves but in God who raises the dead. *2 Cor 1:8-9*

Hail Mary...

Rejoice in hope, endure in affliction, persevere in prayer. *Rom 12:12*

Hail Mary...

[D]raw your strength from the Lord and from his mighty power. *Eph 6:10*

Hail Mary...

If God is for us, who can be against us? *Rom 8:31*

Hail Mary...

[B]y sending his own Son in the likeness of sinful flesh and for the sake of sin, he condemned sin in the flesh, so that the righteous decree of the law might be fulfilled in us, who live not according to the flesh but according to the spirit. *Rom 8:3-4*

Hail Mary...

"In an acceptable time I heard you, / and on the day of salvation I helped you." / Behold, now is a very acceptable time; behold, now is the day of salvation. *2 Cor 6:2*

Hail Mary... Glory Be... O My Jesus...

"Behold, the man!" Jn 19:5
Arch of Ecce Homo
Via Dolorosa, Jerusalem

The Fourth Sorrowful Mystery
The Carrying of the Cross

So they took Jesus, and carrying the cross himself he went out to what is called the Place of the Skull, in Hebrew, Golgotha. ... [S]eek peace and follow after it. *Jn 19:16-17, 1 Pt 3:11*

Our Father...

Station II – Jesus takes up the Cross
Church of the Condemnation and
Imposition of the Cross, Jerusalem

This punishment by the majority is enough for such a person, so that on the contrary you should forgive and encourage him instead, or else the person may be overwhelmed by excessive pain. *2 Cor 2:6-7*

Hail Mary...

"For your sake we are being slain all the day; / we are looked upon as sheep to be slaughtered." *Rom 8:36*

Hail Mary...

We are ... persecuted, but not abandoned; struck down, but not destroyed. *2 Cor 4:8-9*

Hail Mary...

Hence I ask, did they stumble so as to fall? Of course not! *Rom 11:11*

Hail Mary...

Station III – Jesus Falls the First Time
Polish Catholic Chapel, Via Dolorosa, Jerusalem

[Love] bears all things, believes all things, hopes all things, endures all things. *1 Cor 13:7*

Hail Mary...

I consider that the sufferings of this present time are as nothing compared with the glory to be revealed for us. *Rom 8:18*

Hail Mary...

We are afflicted in every way, but not constrained; perplexed, but not driven to despair. *2 Cor 4:8*

Hail Mary...

[W]e also groan within ourselves as we wait for adoption, the redemption of our bodies. For in hope we were saved. *Rom 8:23-24*

Hail Mary...

Station IV — Jesus meets Mary His Mother
Via Dolorosa, Jerusalem

I have the strength for everything through him who empowers me. *Phil 4:13*

Hail Mary...

For this momentary light affliction is producing for us an eternal weight of glory beyond all comparison. *2 Cor 4:17*

Hail Mary... Glory Be... O My Jesus...

Church of the Condemnation and Imposition of the Cross Jerusalem

The Fifth Sorrowful Mystery
The Crucifixion

When they came to the place called the Skull, they crucified him and the criminals there, one on his right, the other on his left. ... He is the image of the invisible God. ... [M]aking peace by the blood of his cross. ... Standing by the cross of Jesus were his mother....
Lk 23:33, Col 1:15,20, Jn 19:25

Our Father...

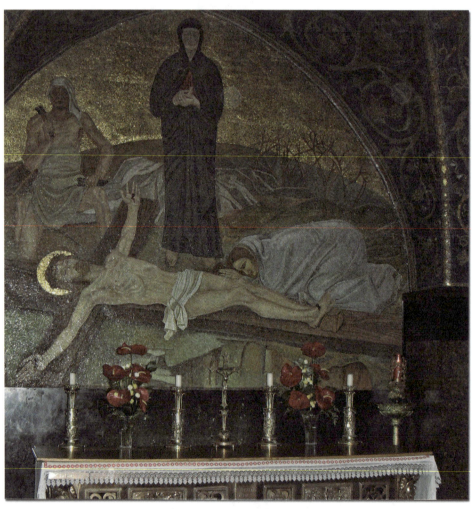

Station XI – Jesus is Nailed to the Cross
Mount Calvary
Church of the Holy Sepulchre, Jerusalem

*Altar at the Site of the Crucifixion
Mount Calvary
Church of the Holy Sepulchre, Jerusalem*

[H]e emptied himself, / taking the form of a slave, / coming in human likeness; / and found human in appearance, / he humbled himself, / becoming obedient to death, / even death on a cross. *Phil 2:7-8*

Hail Mary...

They are justified freely by his grace through the redemption in Christ Jesus, whom God set forth as an expiation, through faith, by his blood, to prove his righteousness because of the forgiveness of sins. *Rom 3:24-25*

Hail Mary...

I urge you therefore, brothers, by the mercies of God, to offer your bodies as a living sacrifice, holy and pleasing to God, your spiritual worship. *Rom 12:1*

Hail Mary...

God proves his love for us in that while we were still sinners Christ died for us. *Rom 5:8*

Hail Mary...

For one believes with the heart and so is justified, and one confesses with the mouth and so is saved. For the scripture says, "No one who believes in him will be put to shame." *Rom 10:10-11*

Hail Mary...

[H]e will continue to rescue us; in him we have put our hope [that] he will also rescue us again. *2 Cor 1:10*

Hail Mary...

Stone of Mount Calvary
Church of the Holy Sepulchre, Jerusalem

[J]ust as through one transgression condemnation came upon all, so through one righteous act acquittal and life came to all. *Rom 5:18*

Hail Mary...

In him we have redemption by his blood, the forgiveness of transgressions, in accord with the riches of his grace that he lavished upon us. *Eph 1:7-8*

Hail Mary...

[F]aith, hope, love remain, these three; but the greatest of these is love. *1 Cor 13:13*

Hail Mary...

Your every act should be done with love. *1 Cor 16:14*

Hail Mary... Glory Be... O My Jesus... Hail Holy Queen...

"Sorrowful Virgin, Patron of Slovakia, Come to Our Aid."
Mosaic from Slovak Republic
Basilica of the Annunciation, Nazareth

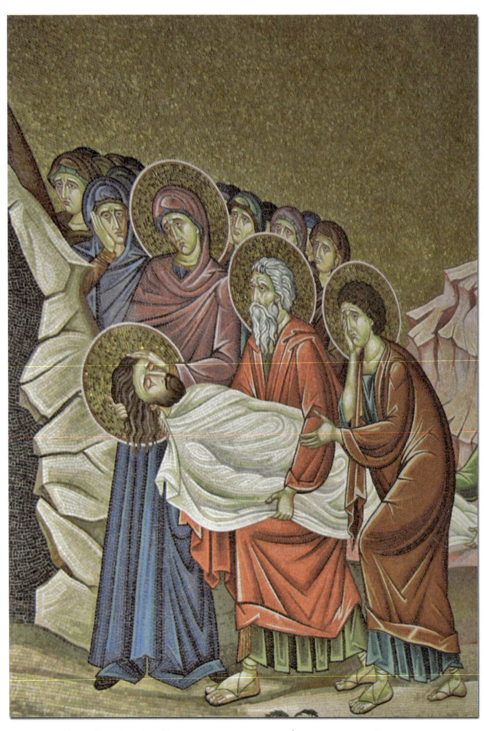

Mural of the Deposition and Anointing of Christ
Church of the Holy Sepulchre, Jerusalem

The Glorious Mysteries

The Sign of the Cross

The Apostles' Creed

[Y]ou are glorifying God for your obedient confession of the gospel of Christ and the generosity of your contribution to them and to all others. ... [T]here will be glory, honor, and peace for everyone who does good. *2 Cor 9:13, Rom 2:10*

Our Father...

I give thanks to my God always, remembering you in my prayers, as I hear of the love and the faith you have in the Lord Jesus and for all the holy ones. *Phlm 4-5*

Hail Mary...

Now hope that sees for itself is not hope. For who hopes for what one sees? *Rom 8:24*

Hail Mary...

God, who is rich in mercy, because of the great love he had for us, even when we were dead in our transgressions, brought us to life with Christ. *Eph 2:4-5*

Hail Mary... Glory Be... O My Jesus...

Tomb of Christ
Church of the Holy Sepulchre, Jerusalem

The First Glorious Mystery
The Resurrection

[H]e took him down, wrapped [Jesus] in the linen cloth and laid him in a tomb that had been hewn out of the rock. Then he rolled a stone against the entrance to the tomb. ... Jesus ... stood in their midst and said, "Peace be with you." Mk 15:46, Jn 20:26

Our Father...

"I am the resurrection and the life. ...
Do you believe this?" Jn 11:25-26
Church of Lazarus, Bethany

[Faith] was also for us, to whom it will be credited, who believe in the one who raised Jesus our Lord from the dead, who was handed over for our transgressions and was raised for our justification. *Rom 4:24-25*

Hail Mary...

Christ died for our sins … was buried … was raised on the third day [and] ... he appeared to Cephas, then to the Twelve. *1 Cor 15:3-5*

Hail Mary...

We were indeed buried with him through baptism into death, so that, just as Christ was raised from the dead by the glory of the Father, we too might live in newness of life. *Rom 6:4*

Hail Mary...

For the gifts and the call of God are irrevocable. *Rom 11:29*

Hail Mary...

We know that all things work for good for those who love God, who are called according to his purpose. *Rom 8:28*

Hail Mary...

[I]f, while we were enemies, we were reconciled to God through the death of his Son, how much more, once reconciled, will we be saved by his life. *Rom 5:10*

Hail Mary...

[H]e was crucified out of weakness, but he lives by the power of God. *2 Cor 13:4*

Hail Mary...

They are justified freely by his grace through the redemption in Christ Jesus. *Rom 3:24*

Hail Mary...

For just as in Adam all die, so too in Christ shall all be brought to life, but each one in proper order: Christ the firstfruits; then, at his coming, those who belong to Christ. *1 Cor 15:22-23*

Hail Mary...

So whoever is in Christ is a new creation: the old things have passed away; behold, new things have come. *2 Cor 5:17*

Hail Mary... Glory Be... O My Jesus...

Jesus came over and took the bread and gave it to them, and in like manner the fish. Jn 21:13
Mensa Christi, Church of the Primacy of Peter
Tabgha, Galilee

The Second Glorious Mystery
The Ascension

Peace I leave with you; my peace I give to you. ... If you loved me, you would rejoice that I am going to the Father. ... "[Y]ou will be my witnesses in Jerusalem, throughout Judea and Samaria, and to the ends of the earth." ... [A]s they were looking on, he was lifted up, and a cloud took him from their sight. *Jn 14:27-28, Acts 1:8-9*

Our Father...

Jesus' right footprint
Chapel of the Ascension
Mount of Olives, Jerusalem

[W]hether we live or die, we are the Lord's. For this is why Christ died and came to life, that he might be Lord of both the dead and the living. *Rom 14:8-9*

Hail Mary...

[W]e look not to what is seen but to what is unseen; for what is seen is transitory, but what is unseen is eternal. *2 Cor 4:18*

Hail Mary...

May the eyes of [your] hearts be enlightened, that you may know ... what is the surpassing greatness of his power ... which he worked in Christ, raising him from the dead and seating him at his right hand in the heavens, far above every principality, authority, power, and dominion. *Eph 1:18-21*

Hail Mary...

[H]e put all things beneath his feet and gave him as head over all things to the church.... *Eph 1:22*

Hail Mary...

What does "he ascended" mean except that he also descended into the lower [regions] of the earth? The one who descended is also the one who ascended far above all the heavens, that he might fill all things. *Eph 4:9-10*

Hail Mary...

"As I live, says the Lord, every knee shall bend before me, / and every tongue shall give praise to God." *Rom 14:11*

Hail Mary...

[A]t the name of Jesus / every knee should bend, / of those in heaven and on earth and under the earth, / and every tongue confess that / Jesus Christ is Lord, / to the glory of God the Father. *Phil 2:10-11*

Hail Mary...

As to his death, he died to sin once and for all; as to his life, he lives for God. *Rom 6:10*

Hail Mary...

[T]hrough whom we have gained access [by faith] to this grace in which we stand, and we boast in hope of the glory of God. *Rom 5:2*

Hail Mary...

To the king of ages, incorruptible, invisible, the only God, honor and glory forever and ever. Amen. *1 Tm 1:17*

Hail Mary... Glory Be... O My Jesus...

*Chapel of the Ascension
Mount of Olives, Jerusalem*

The Third Glorious Mystery
The Descent of the Holy Spirit

When the time for Pentecost was fulfilled, they were all in one place together. And suddenly there came from the sky a noise like a strong driving wind, and it filled the entire house in which they were. Then there appeared to them tongues as of fire, which parted and came to rest on each one of them. ... [P]reserve the unity of the spirit through the bond of peace. *Acts 2:1-3, Eph 4:3*

Our Father...

Pentecost Mosaic
Crypt, Basilica of the Dormition
Mount Zion, Jerusalem

But the one who gives us security with you in Christ and who anointed us is God; he has also put his seal upon us and given the Spirit in our hearts as a first installment. *2 Cor 1:21-22*

Hail Mary...

All of us, gazing with unveiled face on the glory of the Lord, are being transformed into the same image from glory to glory, as from the Lord who is the Spirit. *2 Cor 3:18*

Hail Mary...

[B]e filled with the Spirit, addressing one another [in] psalms and hymns and spiritual songs, singing and playing to the Lord in your hearts. *Eph 5:18-19*

Hail Mary...

We have not received the spirit of the world but the Spirit that is from God, so that we may understand the things freely given us by God. *1 Cor 2:12*

Hail Mary...

[T]he fruit of the Spirit is love, joy, peace, patience, kindness, generosity, faithfulness, gentleness, self-control. *Gal 5:22-23*

Hail Mary...

To each individual the manifestation of the Spirit is given for some benefit. To one is given through the Spirit the expression of wisdom; to another the expression of knowledge according to the same Spirit. *1 Cor 12:7-8*

Hail Mary...

To each individual the manifestation of the Spirit is given for some benefit. ... to another faith by the same Spirit. *1 Cor 12:7,9*

Hail Mary...

I give thanks to my God always ... that your partnership in the faith may become effective in recognizing every good there is in us that leads to Christ. *Phlm 4,6*

Hail Mary...

*Site of the Descent of the Holy Spirit
Outside the Cenacle, Jerusalem*

For the Spirit scrutinizes everything, even the depths of God. *1 Cor 2:10*

Hail Mary...

For God did not give us a spirit of cowardice but rather of power and love and self-control. So do not be ashamed of your testimony to our Lord. *2 Tm 1:7-8*

Hail Mary... Glory Be... O My Jesus...

"[U]pon this rock, I will build my church..." Mt 16:18
Church of St. Peter, Tiberias

The Fourth Glorious Mystery
The Assumption of the
Blessed Virgin Mary into Heaven

May the God of peace himself make you perfectly holy. ... God's temple in heaven was opened, and the ark of his covenant could be seen in the temple. There were flashes of lightning, rumblings, and peals of thunder. ... Mary said: ... / "He has thrown down the rulers from their thrones / but lifted up the lowly."
1 Thes 5:23, Rv 11:19, Lk 1:46, 52

Our Father...

Crypt of the Sleeping Virgin
Basilica of the Dormition
Mt Zion, Jerusalem

Mosaic in Apse
Basilica of the Dormition, Mt Zion, Jerusalem

Greet Mary, who has worked hard for you. *Rom 16:6*

Hail Mary...

[H]e chose us in him, before the foundation of the world, to be holy and without blemish before him. *Eph 1:4*

Hail Mary...

For we are his handiwork, created in Christ Jesus for the good works that God has prepared in advance, that we should live in them. *Eph 2:10*

Hail Mary...

If then you were raised with Christ, seek what is above, where Christ is seated at the right hand of God. Think of what is above, not of what is on earth. *Col 3:1-2*

Hail Mary...

For if we believe that Jesus died and rose, so too will God, through Jesus, bring with him those who have fallen asleep. *1 Thes 4:14*

Hail Mary...

For you have died, and your life is hidden with Christ in God. *Col 3:3*

Hail Mary...

And his heart goes out to you all the more, as he remembers the obedience of all of you, when you received him with fear and trembling. *2 Cor 7:15*

Hail Mary...

Behold, I tell you a mystery. We shall not all fall asleep, but we will all be changed, in an instant, in the blink of an eye, at the last trumpet. For the trumpet will sound, the dead will be raised incorruptible. *1 Cor 15:51-52*

Hail Mary...

[G]ood works are also public; and even those that are not cannot remain hidden. *1 Tm 5:25*

Hail Mary...

Blessed be the God and Father of our Lord Jesus Christ, who has blessed us in Christ with every spiritual blessing in the heavens. *Eph 1:3*

Hail Mary... Glory Be... O My Jesus...

*Basilica of the Dormition
Mt Zion, Jerusalem*

The Fifth Glorious Mystery
The Coronation of Mary,
Queen of Heaven and Earth

I want you to be wise as to what is good, and simple as to what is evil; then the God of peace will crush Satan under your feet. ... A great sign appeared in the sky, a woman clothed with the sun, with the moon under her feet, and on her head a crown of twelve stars. ... Mary said: ... / "For he has looked upon his handmaid's lowliness; / behold, from now on will all ages call me blessed." *Rom 16:19-20, Rv 12:1, Lk 1:46,48*

Our Father...

Church of the Visitation, Ein Karem

If for this life only we have hoped in Christ, we are the most pitiable people of all. *1 Cor 15:19*

Hail Mary...

I continue my pursuit toward the goal, the prize of God's upward calling, in Christ Jesus. *Phil 3:14*

Hail Mary...

I have finished the race; I have kept the faith. From now on the crown of righteousness awaits me, which the Lord, the just judge, will award to me on that day, and not only to me, but to all who have longed for his appearance. *2 Tm 4:7-8*

Hail Mary...

May the God of peace himself make you perfectly holy and may you entirely, spirit, soul, and body, be preserved blameless for the coming of our Lord Jesus Christ. *1 Thes 5:23*

Hail Mary...

"What eye has not seen, and ear has not heard, / and what has not entered the human heart, / what God has prepared for those who love him," *1 Cor 2:9*

Hail Mary...

If we have died with him / we shall also live with him; / if we persevere / we shall also reign with him. *2 Tm 2:11-12*

Hail Mary...

I am confident of this, that the one who began a good work in you will continue to complete it until the day of Christ Jesus. *Phil 1:6*

Hail Mary...

I want you to be wise as to what is good, and simple as to what is evil; then the God of peace will quickly crush Satan under your feet. *Rom 16:19-20*

Hail Mary...

When Christ your life appears, then you too will appear with him in glory. *Col 3:4*

Hail Mary...

Be imitators of me, as I am of Christ. *I Cor 11:1*

Hail Mary... Glory Be... O My Jesus... Hail Holy Queen...

A shoot shall sprout from the stump of Jesse ... Is 11:1
Mosaic of the Tree of Jesse
Basilica of the Dormition, Mt Zion, Jerusalem

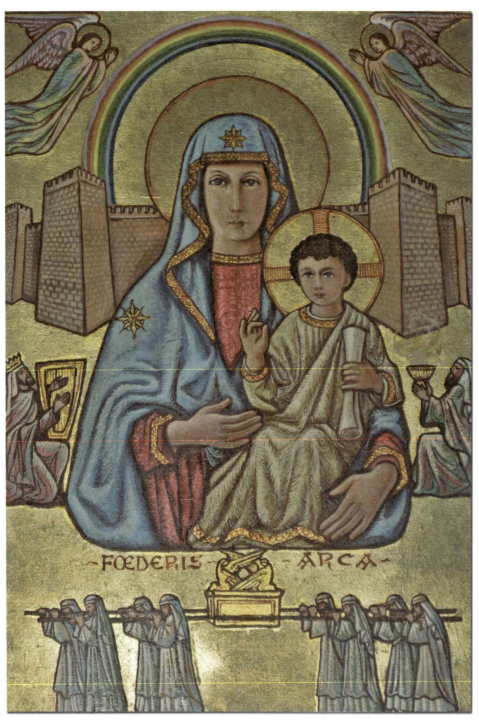

Mary, Mother of God, Ark of the Covenant
Church of Our Lady of the Ark of the Covenant
Abu Gosh (Emmaus)

Notes from the Author

In the 1990s, I wrote <u>From Genesis to Revelation</u> which is a collection of seven scriptural rosaries based on selections from the entirety of Sacred Scriptures. The rosary meditation prayer book was based on thematic collections, such as, the 150 *Psalms*, the Prophets, the Blessed Words of Jesus and Mary, and the writings of St. Paul.

In the 2002 Apostolic Letter *Rosarium Virginis Mariae*, Pope Blessed John Paul II recommended praying a new set of mysteries called the Luminous Mysteries. The Luminous Mysteries filled in the chronological gap from the Fifth Joyful Mystery with Jesus as a boy of twelve to the First Sorrowful Mystery when Jesus begins His Passion in the Agony in the Garden. These Luminous Mysteries complement the Joyful, Sorrowful, and Glorious Mysteries.

I have had many requests to update the Seven Scriptural Rosaries in <u>From Genesis to Revelation</u> with the Luminous Mysteries.

In 2004, <u>The Psalter of Jesus and Mary</u> was the first rosary meditation book to be updated. The Joyful, Sorrowful, and Glorious mysteries remained the same 150 *Psalms*, as presented in <u>From Genesis to Revelation.</u> However, the meditations for the Luminous Mysteries were selected from *Proverbs*, the book that follows *Psalms* in the Bible.

<u>Pearls of Peace</u> is the second rosary meditation book in <u>From Genesis to Revelation</u> to be updated with the Luminous Mysteries. Pope Benedict XVI declared a Jubilee Year of St. Paul from June 2008 through June 2009. It was during that year that the selections for the Luminous Mysteries were completed. The Our Father Scripture meditations highlight the holy places where Jesus lived, preached, taught, and died. Hence, this prayer book is best illustrated with pictures from the Holy Land. When I first saw Father Coulter's photography and his presentation of them with the mysteries of the Most Holy Rosary, I was moved to tears. I trust and pray you will see the beauty in the places of Our Lord and His Blessed Mother by meditating on the mysteries of the Most Holy Rosary.

In closing, I would like to extend a special thank you to Father Michael Duesterhaus, Diocese of Arlington, for his wise counsel. Without his efforts to keep me focused and thinking of the "things above," these prayer books would never have been possible.

Christine Haapala
Fairfax, VA

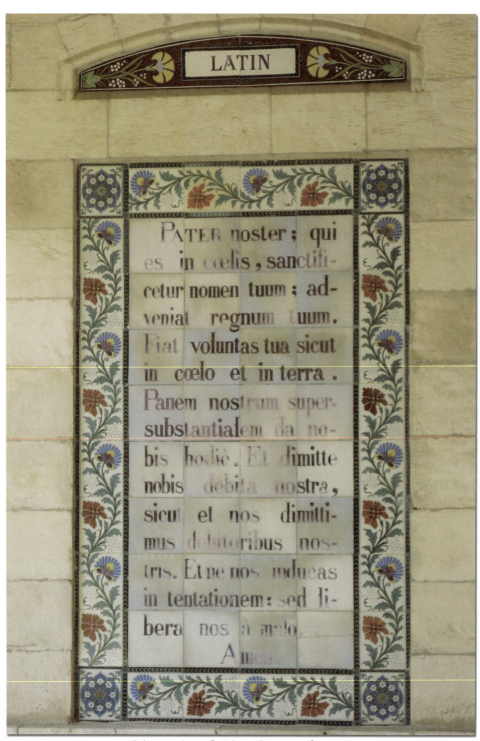

*Church of the Pater Noster
Mount of Olives, Jerusalem*

How to Pray the Most Holy Rosary

While holding the Crucifix in the hand, make the Sign of the Cross and recite the Apostles' Creed. On the first large bead, recite the Our Father. On the three small beads recite the Hail Mary for an increase in the three theological virtues of faith, hope, and love, next pray the Glory Be. Mention each mystery and then recite on the larger bead the Our Father. On the decade of ten small beads meditate on the mystery and recite on each bead the Hail Mary. In closing each decade, recite the Glory Be followed by the O My Jesus prayer. Repeat this sequence of prayers for five decades. Conclude the Most Holy Rosary by praying the Hail Holy Queen.

For many centuries, the Most Holy Rosary was prayed in three sets of mysteries – the Joyful, Sorrowful, and the Glorious. Pope Blessed John Paul II in his Apostolic Letter *Rosarium Virginis Mariae* recommended an additional set of mysteries, the Luminous Mysteries.

While a complete Rosary consists of praying all twenty mysteries, it is more typical of group prayer to only pray five decades at a time. For children or beginners, a five or twenty decade Rosary may be daunting, so begin praying with just one decade. While praying include reading of Sacred Scriptures about each mystery to bring the melody of prayer alive with mental pictures of persons, places, and events.

Originally, the Joyful Mysteries were prayed on Monday and Thursday, the Sorrowful Mysteries on Tuesday and Friday, and the Glorious Mysteries on Wednesday, Saturday, and Sunday. With the addition of the Luminous Mysteries, Pope Blessed John Paul II recommended the Joyful Mysteries be prayed on Saturday and the Luminous Mysteries on Thursday.

The Prayers of the Most Holy Rosary

The Apostles' Creed

I believe in God, the Father almighty, Creator of heaven and earth, and in Jesus Christ, his only Son, our Lord, who was conceived by the Holy Spirit, born of the Virgin Mary, suffered under Pontius Pilate, was crucified, died and was buried; he descended into hell; on the third day he rose again from the dead; he ascended into heaven, and is seated at the right hand of God the Father almighty; from there he will come to judge the living and the dead. I believe in the Holy Spirit, the holy catholic Church, the communion of saints, the forgiveness of sins, the resurrection of the body, and life everlasting. Amen.

Our Father

Our Father, Who art in Heaven, hallowed be Thy Name. Thy kingdom come; Thy will be done on earth as it is in Heaven. Give us this day our daily bread, and forgive us our trespasses, as we forgive those who trespass against us. And lead us not into temptation, but deliver us from evil. Amen.

Hail Mary

Hail Mary, full of grace, the Lord is with thee; blessed art thou among women, and blessed is the Fruit of thy womb, Jesus. Holy Mary, Mother of God, pray for us sinners, now and at the hour of our death. Amen.

Doxology (Glory be)

Glory be to the Father, and to the Son, and to the Holy Spirit. As it was in the beginning, is now, and ever shall be, world without end. Amen

The Fatima Prayer

O My Jesus, forgive us our sins; save us from the fires of Hell, lead all souls to Heaven, especially those who are in most need of Thy Mercy.

Hail Holy Queen

Hail, holy Queen, Mother of mercy, our life, our sweetness and our hope. To thee do we cry, poor banished children of Eve! To thee do we send up our sighs, mourning and weeping in this valley of tears. Turn then, most gracious advocate, thine eyes of mercy towards us. And after this, our exile, show unto us the blessed Fruit of thy womb, Jesus. O clement, O loving, O sweet Virgin Mary.

V. Pray for us, O holy Mother of God
R. That we may be made worthy of the promises of Christ.

Prayer after the Rosary

O God, whose only begotten Son, by His life, death and resurrection, has purchased for us the rewards of eternal life; grant, we beseech Thee, that, meditating upon these mysteries of the Most Holy Rosary of the Blessed Virgin Mary, we may imitate what they contain and obtain what they promise, through the same Christ our Lord. Amen.

Products from Suffering Servant Scriptorium

Prayer Books for Children of All Ages

<u>Speak, Lord, I am Listening</u> A Rosary Book (2nd Ed. with Luminous Mysteries. Includes Study and Discussion Guide) This prayer book presents the richness of the Sacred Mysteries of the Most Holy Rosary in terms that children can visualize and understand. Gus Muller's watercolors use the full palette of color expression to explore the depths of the agony of Christ crucified and reach the heights of the Blessed Virgin Mary's glorious reign as Queen of Heaven and Earth. Succinct and most apt meditation selections yield a wealth of spiritual insight into the mysterious events of the lives of Jesus and Mary. The Scriptures and watercolor illustrations coupled with the prayers of the Most Holy Rosary provide a rich meditation platform for teaching prayer and devotion to Jesus and Mary.

<u>Follow Me</u> A Stations of the Cross Book. Inspired watercolors and selections of God's Word introduce children to the suffering of our Savior Jesus Christ by walking each step with Him to Calvary. Along with each station is a heroically holy person who epitomized self-sacrifice and was beatified or canonized by Pope Blessed John Paul II.

Prayer Books for Adults and Teenagers

<u>Seraphim and Cherubim: A Scriptural Chaplet of the Holy Angels</u> Angels have been with us since the beginning in the "Garden of Eden" and will be with us at the "End of Age." This prayer book joins together Sacred Scripture selections with special invocations to our Blessed Mother and the Holy Archangels. This book includes fabulous full-color pictures from the masters, such as, Raphael, Bruegel the Elder, Perugino and many others. It also includes a newly composed Novena of the Holy Angels and the traditional Litany of the Holy Angels. Those who pray without ceasing and ponder the Good News will find this book equally inspiring and encouraging.

<u>In His Presence: Seven Visits to the Blessed Sacrament</u> This meditation book outlines SEVEN VISITS to the Blessed Sacrament. This prayer book can be used in one evening, such as, during the Holy Thursday Seven Church Pilgrimage. It can be used for seven consecutive days for a special prayer request. And, it can be used periodically, whenever you can spend time visiting Jesus in the Blessed Sacrament.

<u>Psalter of Jesus and Mary</u> This pocket-size Scriptural Rosary prayer book includes the *150 Psalms* Scriptural Rosary for the Joyful, Sorrowful and Glorious Mysteries and meditations for the Luminous Mysteries from *Proverbs*, the wise words of Solomon. The 20 mysteries of the Most Holy Rosary open with a New Testament reflection. There is a short Scripture meditation from either *Psalms* or *Proverbs* for each Hail Mary. An Old and New Testament icon from Julius Schnorr von Carolsfeld's <u>Treasury of Bible Illustrations</u> accompany each mystery.

<u>His Sorrowful Passion</u> This prayer book integrates Sacred Scripture meditations with the prayers of the Chaplet of Divine Mercy. There are two Scriptural Chaplets: one chronicles Jesus' Passion and the other features the Seven Penitential Psalms. The woodcuts of the 15th century Catholic artist, Albrecht Dürer, illustrate this book.

The Suffering Servant's Courage (2nd Ed. with Luminous Mysteries) This prayer book integrates poignant Sacred Scripture verses about courage and fortitude, the prayers of the Most Holy Rosary, and illustrations from the inspired artistry of the 19th century Catholic illustrator Gustave Dóre.

From Genesis to Revelation: Seven Scriptural Rosaries This prayer book is the most thorough and extensive collection of Scriptural Rosaries you will find anywhere. This prayer book goes well beyond the traditional Scriptural Rosary and penetrates the heart of the meditative spirit of the mysteries. It addresses many dimensions: time, from the Old to the New Testament; authors, from Moses, Isaiah, to the Evangelists; and perspectives, from the purely historical to deeper spiritual and prayerful insights. Those who pray the Rosary and those who read the Bible will equally find this prayer book inspirational.

Recorded Prayers available on CD

The Sanctity of Life Scriptural Rosary (2nd Ed. with Luminous Mysteries) Sacred Scripture selections prayed with the Most Holy Rosary uniquely brings you God's message of the dignity and sanctity of life. The prayers are accompanied by meditative piano music. Four different readers lead you in more than two hours of prayerful meditations. Includes four songs from the composer and soprano Nancy Scimone, winner of the UNITY Awards 2002 Best Sacramental Album of the Year for ORA PRO NOBIS. Includes 16-page book with the complete text of the Sacred Scripture selections. Double CD. CD 1 includes the Joyful and Luminous Mysteries and CD 2 includes the Sorrowful and Glorious Mysteries.

Time for Mercy Composer and singer Nancy Scimone offers you a new, spiritually uplifting Chaplet of Divine Mercy melody. This Scriptural Chaplet of Divine Mercy is based on the Penitential Psalm Scriptural Chaplet of Divine Mercy from the book, His Sorrowful Passion. Brother Leonard Konopka, MIC, prays selections from the Seven Penitential Psalms, while Nancy Scimone's crystal clear soprano voice brings us God's message of Divine Mercy.

Quantity orders of Suffering Servant Scriptorium books or CDs may be purchased for liturgical, educational, or sale promotional use. For discount schedule and further information, please call toll free 888-652-9494 or write to us at:

Suffering Servant Scriptorium
Special Market Department
PO Box 1126
Springfield, VA 22151